Playi

Shakespeare's

Hamlet
FOR KIDS
(The melodramatic version!)

For 6-20+ actors, or kids of all ages who want to have fun!
Creatively modified by Brendan P. Kelso
Cover illustrated by Shana Hallmeyer
Cover Character illustrated by Ron Leishman

3 Melodramatic Modifications of Shakespeare's Play
for 3 different group sizes:

6-7+ actors

8-14+ actors

11-20+ actors

Table Of Contents

PlayingWithPlays.com

Dedicated to my buddy Tim Chai; as with Hamlet, a great man passed too young.

-Brendan

For performance rights please see page 6 of this book or contact:

contact@PlayingWithPlays.com

Foreword

When I was in high school there was something about Shakespeare that appealed to me. Not that I understood it mind you, but there were clear scenes and images that always stood out in my mind. Romeo & Juliet, "Romeo, Romeo; wherefore art thou Romeo?"; Julius Caesar, "Et tu Brute"; Macbeth, "Double, Double, toil and trouble"; Hamlet, "to be or not to be"; A Midsummer Night's Dream, all I remember about this was a wickedly cool fairy and something about a guy turning into a donkey that I thought was pretty funny. It was not until I started analyzing Shakespeare's plays as an actor that I realized one very important thing, I still didn't understand them. Seriously though, it's tough enough for adults, let alone kids. Then it hit me, why don't I make a version that kids could perform, but make it easy for them to understand with a splash of Shakespeare lingo mixed in? And voila! A melodramatic masterpiece was created! They are intended to be melodramatically fun!

THE PLAYS: There are 3 plays within this book, for three different group sizes. The reason: to allow educators or parents to get the story across to their children regardless of the size of their group. As you read through the plays, there are several lines that are highlighted. These are actual lines from the original book. I am a little more particular about the kids saying these lines verbatim. But the rest, well... have fun!

The entire purpose of this book is to instill the love of a classic story, as well as drama, into the kids.

And when you have children who have a passion for something, they will start to teach themselves, with or without school.

These plays are intended for pure fun. Please DO NOT have the kids learn these lines verbatim, that would be a complete waste of creativity. But do have them basically know their lines and improvise wherever they want as long as it pertains to telling the story. Because that is the goal of an actor: to tell the story. In A Midsummer Night's Dream, I once had a student playing Quince question me about one of her lines, "but in the actual story, didn't the Mechanicals state that 'they would hang us'?" I thought for a second and realized that she had read the story with her mom, and she was right. So I let her add the line she wanted and it added that much more fun, it made the play theirs. I have had kids throw water on the audience, run around the audience, sit in the audience, lose their pumpkin pants (size 30 around a size 15 doesn't work very well, but makes for some great humor!) and most importantly, die all over the stage. The kids love it.

One last note: if you want some educational resources, loved our plays, want to tell the world how much your kids loved performing Shakespeare, want to insult someone with our Shakespeare Insult Generator, or are just a fan of Shakespeare, then hop on our website and have fun:

PlayingWithPlays.com

With these notes, I'll see you on the stage, have fun, and break a leg!

SCHOOL, AFTERSCHOOL, and SUMMER classes

I've been teaching these plays as afterschool and summer programs for quite some time. Many people have asked what the program is, therefore, I have put together a basic formula so any teacher or parent can follow and have melodramatic success! As well, many teachers use my books in a variety of ways. You can view the formula and many more resources on my website at: PlayingWithPlays.com

- Brendan

OTHER PLAYS AND FULL LENGTH SCRIPTS

We have over 25 different titles, as well as a full-length play in 4-acts for theatre groups: Shakespeare's Hilarious Tragedies. You can see all of our other titles on our website here: PlayingWithPlays.com/books

As well, you can see a sneak peek at some of those titles at the back of this book.

And, if you ever have any questions, please don't hesitate to ask at: Contact@PlayingWithPlays.com

ROYALTIES

If you have any questions about royalties or performance licenses, here are the basic guidelines:

1) Please contact us! We always LOVE to hear about a school or group performing our books! We would also love to share photos and brag about your program as well! (with your permission, of course)

2) If you are a group and DO NOT charge your kids to be in this production, contact us about discounted copyright fees (one way or another, we will make this work for you!) You are NOT required to buy a book per kid (but, we will still send you some really cool Shakespeare tattoos for your kids!)

3) If you are a group and DO charge your kids to be in the production, (i.e. afterschool program, summer camp) we ask that you purchase a book per kid. Contact us as we will give you a bulk discount (10 books or more) and send some really cool press on Shakespeare tattoos!

4) If you are a group and DO NOT charge the audience to see the plays, please see our website FAQs to see if you are eligible to waive the performance royalties (most performances are eligible).

5) If you are a group and DO charge the audience to see the performance, please see our website FAQs for performance licensing fees (this includes performances for donations and competitions).

Any other questions or comments, please see our website or email us at:

contact@PlayingWithPlays.com

The 15-Minute or so Hamlet

By William Shakespeare
Creatively modified by Brendan P. Kelso
6-7+ Actors

CAST OF CHARACTERS:

HAMLET: son to the dead King Hamlet, nephew to Claudius, the thinker, or "over" thinker (he's complicated)

CLAUDIUS: the big, bad new King of Denmark

GERTRUDE: Queen, Hamlet's mom, married to his dad & then to his uncle (it's complicated)

POLONIUS: a lord (bad guy too!)

OPHELIA: Polonius' daughter, thinks Hamlet is cute!

[1]LAERTES: Polonius' son and sword-fighter, thinks Hamlet is rotten!

[1]GHOST: a ghost, duh

ONLOOKERS: (extras, as many as needed)

The same actors can play the following parts:
[1]LAERTES and GHOST

ACT 1 SCENE 1

(enter GHOST wandering on stage in ghostly fashion, maybe creeps through audience)

GHOST: *(waits a few seconds, then tries to scare audience)* BOO!

(GHOST exits)

(enter CLAUDIUS and GERTRUDE)

CLAUDIUS: *(to the audience)* I love being the ruler! *(HAMLET enters)* Hey, Hamlet, my new son, why are you looking so down in the dumps?

HAMLET: *(to audience while pointing at Claudius)* A little more than kin, and less than kind. *(to Claudius)* Oh, I'm just bummed that my dad died and my mom married my uncle the very next day...ohh, excuse me...I mean YOU!

GERTRUDE: Dear, stop being such a drag. All that lives must die. You know... the circle of life, or haven't you heard?

HAMLET: Whatever, Mom. That it should come to this! He is my father's brother, but no more like my father than I to Hercules! I'm going to see my friends.

(GERTRUDE and CLAUDIUS exit)

HAMLET: I thought I saw my father in a dream the other night, in my mind's eye. I'll stop by tonight and check it out!

(ALL exit)

ACT 1 SCENE 3

(LAERTES, OPHELIA, and POLONIUS enter)

LAERTES: Ophelia, sis, please stop hanging out with Hamlet. That prince is a bit crazy.

OPHELIA: But I love him!

LAERTES: Whoa, remember, this is a tragedy, not a fairy tale. Most people die in tragedies, especially people who love the main character.

POLONIUS: Laertes, aren't you supposed to be going back to France?

LAERTES: Oh yeah, see ya, Dad! *(LAERTES exits)*

POLONIUS: *(to LAERTES as he leaves)* Hey! Neither a borrower nor a lender be!

LAERTES: What?

POLONIUS: Just giving you some advice about money!

LAERTES: *(a bit confused)* Oh. Okay. Later!

POLONIUS: *(to OPHELIA)* Your brother is right, Hamlet is crazy.

OPHELIA: But, I so totally like him!

POLONIUS: I forbid you to see him!

OPHELIA: I shall obey, Dad. I mean, I so totally DON'T like him anymore.

POLONIUS: Good! *(POLONIUS exits)*

OPHELIA: *(OPHELIA to audience)* I'm a teenager, like I'm going to listen to my dad!

(OPHELIA exits)

(HAMLET enters)

HAMLET: Something is rotten in the state of Denmark. Okay, I'm here. Now, where is this ghost of my dad I heard stopped by?

(GHOST sneaks up behind HAMLET)

GHOST: Boo!

HAMLET: Aghhhhh!

GHOST: Hah! Scared ya!

HAMLET: Who are you?

GHOST: *(in a ghostly voice)* I am your father's spirit.

HAMLET: Oh. ....What!?

GHOST: Your father, you know, the ex-King! I want you to know that the serpent that did sting thy father's life now wears his crown.

HAMLET: What?

GHOST: I was the King until your Uncle Claudius poisoned me by pouring icky stuff in my ear! Murder most foul!

HAMLET: Uncle Claudius killed you?

GHOST: Yeah, then he married my wife, YOUR MOM, and then became King!

HAMLET: WHAT!?! Ohhh, that makes me soooo mad!

GHOST: Yeah? Well, how do you think I feel? Dead and all.... O horrible, O horrible, most horrible.

HAMLET: Yeah, guess that stinks too. So what do you want me to do?

GHOST: Avenge me! You MUST kill Claudius!

HAMLET: Whoa! Kill Claudius? Well.....ahhh....not really sure I like that, I mean, it's just not right, killing someone. What if you don't really exist?

GHOST: Did you not hear me? He killed me, married your mom, and is now the new King. Doesn't that make you a bit angry?

HAMLET: *(getting riled up)* Yeah.

GHOST: I am your father, don't you want to avenge my death?

HAMLET: *(getting more riled up)* YEAH!

GHOST: Then get going!

HAMLET: I WILL AVENGE YOU, FATHER!

GHOST: Oh, and Hamlet?

HAMLET: YEAH?

GHOST: Boo! *(HAMLET jumps up scared)*

HAMLET: Quit doing that!

GHOST: Sorry son, it's one of the perks of the job. My hour is almost come, now get going! *(now in a ghostly voice)* AVENGE ME!

(GHOST exits)

HAMLET: *(to exiting ghost)* Rest, rest, perturbed spirit!

(HAMLET exits)

(enter OPHELIA and POLONIUS)

OPHELIA: Dad, Hamlet is looking a bit weird lately. I mean, his clothes are ragged and he is talking to himself...not quite as cute as he once was, but I still like him!

POLONIUS: I told you to stay away from him!

OPHELIA: I did!

POLONIUS: Hamlet is probably crazy without your love! That hath made him mad. *(to audience)* I will tell Claudius the king!

(ALL exit)

(enter CLAUDIUS, GERTRUDE, and POLONIUS)

GERTRUDE: Claudius, we need to find out why Hamlet is acting so strange lately. I beseech you instantly to visit my too much changed son, Hamlet.

POLONIUS: *(to CLAUDIUS)* Sir, I have found the very cause of Hamlet's lunacy. I know why he has been acting so crazy!

GERTRUDE: Why!?

POLONIUS: I will be brief. Your noble son is mad. He is in love with Ophelia and I have told her to reject him! Claudius, why don't we spy on him?

CLAUDIUS: Sounds like fun! But what if he is faking being crazy?

POLONIUS: Hmmm. Though this be madness, yet there is method in't.

CLAUDIUS: Right?

(exit CLAUDIUS, POLONIUS, and GERTRUDE; enter HAMLET)

HAMLET: *(to audience)* Ah ha! I have an idea! I hear there are some actors coming to do a play before the king. The play's the thing, wherein I'll catch the conscience of the king. I will have the players act out how my father was killed! Then Claudius will feel guilty and admit his crime! Oh, vengeance! Claudius is a bloody, bawdy villain! Remorseless, treacherous, lecherous, kindless villain!

(HAMLET exits)

(enter HAMLET)

HAMLET: To be, or not to be, that is the question. *(to audience)* Really...that *is* the question, and if any of you have the answer, I would really appreciate a little help here.

(enter OPHELIA)

OPHELIA: Hello, Ham.

HAMLET: Hello, O.

OPHELIA: So, whatcha been up to?

HAMLET: Just contemplating life and talking to myself again. Hey, you know I like you?

OPHELIA: Really?

HAMLET: Ahhhh, no.

OPHELIA: You are sooooo mean!

HAMLET: I don't like you at all! Get thee to a nunnery!

OPHELIA: O, woe is me! *(OPHELIA exits as she is crying with a really bad fake cry)*

HAMLET: Whatever. Now let me think of another great speech, oh yeah, *(as HAMLET exits)* What dreams may come, when we blah, blah, blah.....

(HAMLET exits)

(enter HAMLET)

HAMLET: *(to audience)* Now watch Claudius closely during the play, he will show his guilt and that will prove he killed my father! Boy, I hope they remember to suit the action to the word, the word to the action. I know, I know *(using air quotes)* "be careful Hamlet". I know I should be worried, because this is a tragedy, and the main character usually dies in a tragedy, and, yes, I am the main character! But, *(getting a little crazy)* I MUST PROVE HE KILLED MY FATHER!

HAMLET: *(looking offstage)* Oh look, they're starting the play.

(enter CLAUDIUS, very angry)

CLAUDIUS: STOP! Give me some light, away! That play is HORRIBLE!

(CLAUDIUS exits)

HAMLET: I was right! *(does a happy dance)*

HAMLET: *(to audience)* I need to see my mother! I will speak daggers to her but use none. I am MAD! MAD, I tell you!!!!

(HAMLET exits screaming about being mad!)

(enter CLAUDIUS)

CLAUDIUS: *(to audience)* I feel realllllllly bad about killing my brother, King Hamlet. I think I will pray about it. Yeah, that will make me feel better! *(he kneels and starts praying; enter HAMLET)*

HAMLET: *(seeing CLAUDIUS and addressing audience)* What's this? *(starts pulling out his sword)* And now I'll do it! And so I am revenged! *(talking to himself)* But he can't fight back, so it's not fair. Oh, darn it! I hate having a conscience, it's so inconvenient! I am so confused!

(HAMLET exits)

CLAUDIUS: *(to audience)* Well, I don't know about you, but I feel refreshed!

(CLAUDIUS exits)

(enter GERTRUDE and POLONIUS)

GERTRUDE: What's up, Polonius?

POLONIUS: I am going to hide and spy on your conversation with Hamlet!

GERTRUDE: Oh, okay.

(POLONIUS hides somewhere, enter HAMLET very mad, swinging his sword around)

HAMLET: MOM!!! I AM VERY MAD!

GERTRUDE: Ahhh! You scared me!

(POLONIUS sneezes from hiding spot)

HAMLET: *(not seeing POLONIUS)* How now, a rat? Who's hiding? *(stabs POLONIUS)*

POLONIUS: O, I am slain! Ohhhh, the pain! *(dies on stage)*

GERTRUDE: Oh me, what has thou done?

HAMLET: Oops, I thought that was Claudius. Hmph, oh well... as I was saying, I AM MAD you married uncle Claudius!

GERTRUDE: Oh that, yeah, sorry. *(in a motherly voice)* Now, you just killed Polonius, clean up this mess and go to your room!

HAMLET: Okay Mom. *(mimicking his mom in her voice)* Clean up this mess and go to your room.

(ALL exit, HAMLET drags POLONIUS' body offstage)

(enter GERTRUDE and CLAUDIUS)

GERTRUDE: Ahhh, Dear?

CLAUDIUS: Yeah?

GERTRUDE: Ummmm, you would not believe what I have seen tonight! Polonius is dead.

CLAUDIUS: WHAT!?

GERTRUDE: Yeah, Hamlet was acting a little crazy, Polonius sneezed or something, then Hamlet yelled, "A rat, a rat!" and then WHACK! It was over.

CLAUDIUS: *(very angry)* HAMLET!!!! GET OVER HERE NOW!!!!!

(enter HAMLET)

CLAUDIUS: *(very casual)* Hey, what's up?

HAMLET: What noise, who calls on Hamlet? What do you want?

CLAUDIUS: Now, Hamlet. Where's Polonius' body?

HAMLET: I'm not telling!

CLAUDIUS: Oh come on, please tell me!!! Please! With a cherry on top! Where is Polonius?

HAMLET: Oh, all right. He's over there, up the stairs into the lobby. *(points offstage)*

(POLONIUS enters and dies again)

CLAUDIUS: Ewe... he's a mess! Hamlet, I am sending you off to England.

HAMLET: Fine! Farewell, dear Mother. And I'm taking this with me! *(drags POLONIUS' body offstage)*

(ALL exit but CLAUDIUS)

CLAUDIUS: *(to audience)* I have arranged his execution in England! *(laughs evilly as he exits)* Muahahaha....

ACT 4 SCENE 4

(enter HAMLET addresses audience – obviously very upset)

HAMLET: I am suddenly feeling very upset! This play is lasting really long. I need to speed this revenge thing up! Don't you all agree? *(audience will quietly answer yes)*

HAMLET: *(yelling backstage)* HEY, DO YOU ALL AGREE?

(everyone answers backstage, "YES!")

(CLAUDIUS pokes his head out)

CLAUDIUS: Ahhh, excuse me, I'm not so sure I agree....

HAMLET: *(pointing sword at CLAUDIUS)* Go away!

(ALL exit)

(enter OPHELIA and GERTRUDE)

GERTRUDE: Hey Ophelia, you feeling okay?

OPHELIA: *(acting a little crazy)* I am really feeling weird right now.

(OPHELIA wandering around stage doing weird and crazy things; enter CLAUDIUS)

CLAUDIUS: *(staring at OPHELIA)* She is acting really weird. Is she okay?

GERTRUDE: Well think about it; her father just got killed by her boyfriend, whom she just broke up with, yet is still in love with. How would you feel?

CLAUDIUS: Oh, no wonder she is kind of wacky.

(enter LAERTES very upset)

LAERTES: Where is this king? *(noticing CLAUDIUS)* WHAT HAPPENED TO MY FATHER, *(noticing OPHELIA acting crazy)* and why is my sister looking so... loony?

GERTRUDE: Well, as I was telling Claudius, she's a bit bummed that her boyfriend killed your dad.

LAERTES: Aghhhhhhh!!! I will have REVENGE!

CLAUDIUS: Laertes, my friend, look, I will help you get your revenge. I pray you go with me.

(GERTRUDE and OPHELIA exit)

CLAUDIUS: Listen, Hamlet killed your father and wants to kill you too!

LAERTES: Ohhhh, he thinks so! I will get him!

CLAUDIUS: Let's make an evil plan!

LAERTES: Sounds great!

(CLAUDIUS and LAERTES laugh evilly together)

CLAUDIUS: How about you and Hamlet have a sword fight? And Hamlet's sword is blunt?

LAERTES: Great! And I will put poison on my tip to make sure he dies!

CLAUDIUS: Great! And I will put poison in his drink if none of that works!

LAERTES & CLAUDIUS: GREAT!

(they high five; enter GERTRUDE)

GERTRUDE: What are you two up to?

LAERTES & CLAUDIUS: Nothing. *(laughing to each other)*

GERTRUDE: Well, then. Ahhh, Laertes? I have some bad news.

LAERTES: Really? I have had enough of that, can I have some good news?

GERTRUDE: Nope, Ophelia just drowned. *(GERTRUDE drags OPHELIA'S body on stage – head soaking wet if possible!)*

LAERTES: WHAT!? Drown'd! O, where?

GERTRUDE: Yeah, outside...in water...sorry.

LAERTES: Alas, then, she is drown'd?

OPHELIA: *(looks up at audience)* Drowned!

GERTRUDE: Drown'd, drown'd.

LAERTES: I am sooooo going to get Hamlet!!!!

(LAERTES runs offstage waving his sword; ALL exit GERTRUDE drags OPHELIA offstage)

(HAMLET enters, finds a skull on stage)

HAMLET: Oh look, a skull. Wow, it's from this grave marked Yorick. YORICK! Alas, poor Yorick! I knew him. When I was a kid, he was the jester, the funniest guy I knew. So full of life and now he's.....dead. Bummer.

(enter LAERTES, GERTRUDE, and CLAUDIUS)

HAMLET: *(to audience)* Oh look! Hide! *(HAMLET goes off to side of stage)*

GERTRUDE: We must bury Ophelia.

LAERTES: *(starts weeping and crying extremely loud)* I AM SOOOOO MAD AT HAMLET!!! It's his fault my sister and father are dead!

(HAMLET jumps up to confront LAERTES)

HAMLET: Laertes, I loved Ophelia, how dare you say I killed her!

LAERTES: Aghhhhhh! *(charges at HAMLET and they start to fight)*

(CLAUDIUS pulls back LAERTES)

CLAUDIUS: STOP! We will resolve this with the swordfight!

(ALL exit)

(enter HAMLET with a scroll or paper of some sort)

HAMLET: The king has placed a wager that I cannot beat Laertes in a swordfight! What!?! Bring it on! *(talks to audience)*

I know, I know, this is a tragedy, main character usually dies, blah, blah, blah...

(enter LAERTES, GERTRUDE, CLAUDIUS, and other on-lookers)

HAMLET: So, I hear you want to fight?

LAERTES: Yeah, you killed my father... and sister, prepare to die!

HAMLET: Look, I really didn't mean to kill your father. He sneezed and freaked me out.

LAERTES: *(handing sword to HAMLET)* Just take your sword and let's go.

(CLAUDIUS and LAERTES to the side)

CLAUDIUS: Is your sword poisoned?

LAERTES: Yep. Is your wine poisoned?

CLAUDIUS: You betcha! *(to audience, while ALL watch him)* If Hamlet wins, we will all drink wine! *(winks at audience while holding up poisoned wine cup)*

(LAERTES and HAMLET start to fight, HAMLET strikes first)

LAERTES: Ouch! That hurt!

HAMLET: How about this! *(strikes him again)*

LAERTES: Hey! *(strikes back and hits HAMLET)*

HAMLET: Ouch!

GERTRUDE: All this fighting is making me thirsty! *(drinks poisoned wine)*

CLAUDIUS: GERTRUDE, do not drink! *(to audience)* It is the poisoned cup. It's too late. Oh well, on with the fight!

(during fight, HAMLET and LAERTES manage to drop and switch swords – this must be obvious to the audience)

LAERTES: *(to CLAUDIUS)* He has MY SWORD!

CLAUDIUS: Well, don't get hit!

(HAMLET strikes LAERTES again)

LAERTES: Noooooooooo!!!!!!!

(GERTRUDE suddenly gets up and starts to die)

HAMLET: MOMMY!!!! Aghhhhhhh!!!!

GERTRUDE: O my dear Hamlet. The drink, the drink, I am poison'd *(dies in melodramatic fashion, ALL watch)*

HAMLET: *(very mad)* Oh villainy! Ho, let the door be lock'd! Treachery! Seek it out!

(LAERTES starts dying)

LAERTES: Hamlet. Listen, Claudius poisoned the wine cup and your mom drank it. He also poisoned my sword.

HAMLET: Oh, that's not good.

LAERTES: Nope, we're both going to die. The king, the king's to blame. I am justly killed with my own treachery!

(LAERTES falls over dead)

CLAUDIUS: *(to audience)* Don't you just hate tattletales!

HAMLET: CLAUDIUS!!!! *(HAMLET chases CLAUDIUS around stage and finally kills him)*

HAMLET: *(starting to die)* Well, this did not turn out as I expected! I guess this was a tragedy after all! O, I die. The rest is silence.

(HAMLET dies melodramatically)

(ALL exit)

THE END

NOTES

The 20-Minute or so Hamlet

By William Shakespeare
Creatively modified by Brendan P. Kelso
8-14+ Actors

CAST OF CHARACTERS:

HAMLET: son to the dead King Hamlet, nephew to Claudius, the thinker, or "over" thinker (he's complicated)

CLAUDIUS: the big, bad new King of Denmark

GERTRUDE: Queen, Hamlet's mom, married to his dad & then to his uncle (it's complicated)

²POLONIUS: a lord (bad guy too!)

OPHELIA: Polonius' daughter, thinks Hamlet is cute!

LAERTES: Polonius' son and sword-fighter, thinks Hamlet is rotten!

³ROSENCRANTZ: crazy guy #1

¹GUILDENSTERN: crazy guy #2

¹HORATIO: Hamlet's closest friend

³GHOST: a ghost, duh

³PLAYER: an actor

³OSRIC: a young dude

²FORTINBRAS: Prince of Norway

²SAILOR: a sailor

ON-LOOKERS: (extras, as many as needed)

The same actors can play the following parts:
¹HORATIO and GUILDENSTERN
²POLONIUS, SAILOR, and FORTINBRAS
³GHOST, PLAYER, ROSENCRANTZ, and OSRIC

ACT 1 SCENE 1

(enter HORATIO)

HORATIO: *(to the audience)* I hear there is a ghost out tonight. Where is he? *(calling out and whistling)* Here, ghosty, ghosty, here boy!

(enter GHOST from behind HORATIO)

GHOST: *(sneaking up behind HORATIO)* Boo!

(HORATIO screams frantically)

HORATIO: That is NOT funny! *(to the audience)*

GHOST: Ahhh, yes it is!

HORATIO: NO, it is not!

GHOST: Whatever, dude. *(continues wondering around)*

HORATIO: *(to the audience)* Is it not like the King? I must tell Hamlet! He'll know what to do!

(ALL exit)

(enter CLAUDIUS and GERTRUDE)

CLAUDIUS: *(to the audience)* I love being the ruler! *(HAMLET enters)* Hey Hamlet, my new son, why are you looking so down in the dumps?

HAMLET: *(to audience while pointing at Claudius)* A little more than kin, and less than kind. *(to Claudius)* Oh, I'm just bummed that my dad died and my mom married my uncle the very next day...ohh, excuse me...I mean YOU!

GERTRUDE: Dear, stop being such a drag. All that lives must die. You know... the circle of life, or haven't you heard?

HAMLET: Whatever, Mom. That it should come to this! He is my father's brother, but no more like my father than I to Hercules! I'm going to see my friends.

(GERTRUDE, CLAUDIUS exit; HORATIO enters)

HORATIO: Hamlet, I saw your dad last night as a ghost!

HAMLET: No way!

HORATIO: Way!

HAMLET: I thought I saw him in a dream the other night, in my mind's eye. I'll stop by tonight and check it out!

(ALL exit)

ACT 1 SCENE 3

(LAERTES, OPHELIA, and POLONIUS enter)

LAERTES: Ophelia, sis, please stop hanging out with Hamlet. That prince is a bit crazy.

OPHELIA: But I love him!

LAERTES: Whoa, remember, this is a tragedy, not a fairy tale. Most people die in tragedies, especially people who love the main character.

POLONIUS: Laertes, aren't you supposed to be going back to France?

LAERTES: Oh yeah, see ya, Dad! *(LAERTES exits)*

POLONIUS: *(to LAERTES as he leaves)* Hey! Neither a borrower nor a lender be!

LAERTES: What?

POLONIUS: Just giving you some advice about money!

LAERTES: *(a bit confused)* Oh. Okay. Later!

POLONIUS: *(to OPHELIA)* Your brother is right, Hamlet is crazy.

OPHELIA: But, I so totally like him!

POLONIUS: I forbid you to see him!

OPHELIA: I shall obey, Dad. I mean, I so totally DON'T like him anymore.

POLONIUS: Good! *(POLONIUS exits)*

OPHELIA: *(OPHELIA to audience)* I'm a teenager, like I'm going to listen to my dad!

(OPHELIA exits)

(HAMLET and HORATIO enter)

HORATIO: *(to the audience)* Something is rotten in the state of Denmark.

HAMLET: Okay, I'm here. Now, where is this ghost of my dad you have been talking about?

(HORATIO is looking around; GHOST enters)

HORATIO: There he is!

HAMLET: Where?

(GHOST sneaks up behind HAMLET)

GHOST: Boo!

HAMLET: Aghhhhh!

GHOST: Hah! Scared ya!

HAMLET: Who are you?

GHOST: *(in a ghostly voice)* I am your father's spirit.

HAMLET: Oh. ....What!?

GHOST: Your father, you know, the ex-King! I want you to know that the serpent that did sting thy father's life now wears his crown.

HAMLET: What?

GHOST: I was the King until your Uncle Claudius poisoned me by pouring icky stuff in my ear! Murder most foul!

HAMLET: Uncle Claudius killed you?

GHOST: Yeah, then he married my wife, YOUR MOM, and then became King!

HAMLET: WHAT?! Ohhh, that makes me soooo mad!

GHOST: Yeah? Well, how do you think I feel? Dead and all.... O horrible, O horrible, most horrible.

HAMLET: Yeah, guess that stinks too. So what do you want me to do?

GHOST: Avenge me! You MUST kill Claudius!

HAMLET: Whoa! Kill Claudius? Well.....ahhh....not really sure I like that, I mean, it's just not right, killing someone. What if you don't really exist?

GHOST: Did you not hear me? He killed me, married your mom, and is now the new king. Doesn't that make you a bit angry?

HAMLET: *(getting riled up)* Yeah.

GHOST: I am your father, don't you want to avenge my death!

HAMLET: *(getting more riled up)* YEAH!

GHOST: Then get going!

HAMLET: I WILL AVENGE YOU, FATHER!

GHOST: Oh, and Hamlet?

HAMLET: YEAH?

GHOST: Boo! *(HAMLET jumps up scared)*

HAMLET: Quit doing that!

GHOST: Sorry son, it's one of the perks of the job. My hour is almost come, now get going! *(now in a ghostly voice)* AVENGE ME!

(GHOST exits)

HAMLET: *(to exiting ghost)* Rest, Rest, perturbed spirit!

(ALL exit)

(enter OPHELIA and POLONIUS)

OPHELIA: Dad, Hamlet is looking a bit weird lately. I mean, his clothes are ragged and he is talking to himself...not quite as cute as he once was, but I still like him!

POLONIUS: I told you to stay away from him!

OPHELIA: I did!

POLONIUS: Hamlet is probably crazy without your love! That hath made him mad. *(to audience)* I will tell Claudius the king!

(ALL exit)

ACT 2 SCENE 2

(enter CLAUDIUS, ROSENCRANTZ, GUILDENSTERN, and GERTRUDE)

CLAUDIUS: Rosencrantz and Guildenstern?

ROSENCRANTZ & GUILDENSTERN: Yes sir!

CLAUDIUS: I need you to take on a very, very, very, very, very, very secret mission!

ROSENCRANTZ: Secret mission? Yes sir!

GUILDENSTERN: We get to be spies?

ROSENCRANTZ: I want to be the spy!

GUILDENSTERN: *(starting an argument with ROSENCRANTZ)* No, I'm the spy!

ROSENCRANTZ: NO, I'm the spy!

GUILDENSTERN: NO! I'M THE SPY!

CLAUDIUS: Stop!

ROSENCRANTZ & GUILDENSTERN: Sorry, sir.

GUILDENSTERN: *(whispering to ROSENCRANTZ)* I'm still the spy!

GERTRUDE: We need you to find out why Hamlet is acting so strange lately. I beseech you instantly to visit my too much changed son, Hamlet.

GUILDENSTERN: We will do whatever it takes.

ROSENCRANTZ: Hey, that's my line.

GUILDENSTERN: No, it's my line.

ROSENCRANTZ: No, It's MY line!

GUILDENSTERN: NO, IT'S MY LINE!!!

CLAUDIUS: Stop!

ROSENCRANTZ & GUILDENSTERN: Sorry, sir.

ROSENCRANTZ: By the way, is there any money in it for us?

CLAUDIUS: Sure, here's a dollar.

ROSENCRANTZ: *(takes dollar)* It's mine!

GUILDENSTERN: *(starting an argument with ROSENCRANTZ)* No, it's mine!

ROSENCRANTZ: No, mine!

GUILDENSTERN: NO! MINE!

CLAUDIUS: *(annoyed by them)* Here's another dollar, just go!

(ROSENCRANTZ & GUILDENSTERN exit still arguing; enter POLONIUS)

POLONIUS: *(to CLAUDIUS)* Sir, I have found the very cause of Hamlet's lunacy. I know why he has been acting so crazy!

GERTRUDE: Why!?

POLONIUS: I will be brief. Your noble son is mad. He is in love with Ophelia and I have told her to reject him! Claudius, why don't we spy on him?

CLAUDIUS: Sounds like fun! But what if he is faking being crazy?

POLONIUS: Hmmm. Though this be madness, yet there is method in't.

CLAUDIUS: Right?

(exit CLAUDIUS, POLONIUS, and GERTRUDE; enter HAMLET, ROSENCRANTZ & GUILDENSTERN)

ROSENCRANTZ: What's up, Ham?

GUILDENSTERN: How have you been, buddy?

HAMLET: Oh, just thinking.

ROSENCRANTZ: 'Bout what?

HAMLET: Well, since you asked. Did you know there is nothing either good or bad, but thinking makes it so?

GUILDENSTERN: *(ROSENCRANTZ & GUILDENSTERN looking at each other with a puzzled look on their faces)* Man, you are a weird dude.

HAMLET: Whatever. What brings you around here?

ROSENCRANTZ: My lord, we were sent for, by the king. By the way, there are some players coming into town today, you should check them out.

HAMLET: *(to audience)* Ah haa! I have an idea! The play's the thing. Wherein I'll catch the conscience of the king. I will have the players act out how my father was killed! Then Claudius will feel guilty and admit his crime! Oh, vengeance! Claudius is a bloody, bawdy villain! Remorseless, treacherous, lecherous, kindless villain!

(ALL exit but HAMLET, who addresses audience)

HAMLET: What luck to find these actors! It will be great to see Claudius show his guilt! What a piece of work is a man!

(HAMLET exits)

(enter HAMLET)

HAMLET: To be, or not to be, that is the question *(to audience)* Really...that *is* the question, and if any of you have the answer, I would really appreciate a little help here.

(enter OPHELIA)

OPHELIA: Hello, Ham.

HAMLET: Hello, O.

OPHELIA: So, whatcha been up to?

HAMLET: Just contemplating life and talking to myself again. Hey, you know I like you?

OPHELIA: Really?

HAMLET: Ahhhh, no.

OPHELIA: You are sooooo mean!

HAMLET: I don't like you at all! Get thee to a nunnery!

OPHELIA: O, woe is me! *(OPHELIA exits as she is crying with a really bad fake cry)*

HAMLET: Whatever. Now let me think of another great speech, oh yeah, *(as HAMLET exits)* What dreams may come, when we blah, blah, blah.....

(HAMLET exits)

(enter HAMLET, PLAYER, and HORATIO)

PLAYER: *(to Hamlet)* I will do the play just as you wrote it!

(PLAYER off to side practicing acting)

HAMLET: Horatio, now watch Claudius closely during the play, he will show his guilt and that will prove he killed my father! Hey... *(to the PLAYER)* Suit the action to the word, the word to the action.

PLAYER: Right!

HORATIO: Ahh, you do realize this is a tragedy, right?

HAMLET: Yeah, why?

HORATIO: Well, I just want you to know that usually, in a tragedy, the main character gets killed in the end.

HAMLET: So, what's your point?

HORATIO: YOU are the main character, they even named the play after you: "HAMLET," so BE CAREFUL!

HAMLET: *(getting a little crazy)* Yeah, well, I MUST PROVE HE KILLED MY FATHER!

HORATIO: Okey-dokey. Don't say I didn't warn ya. Here they come!

(enter CLAUDIUS, GERTRUDE, and OPHELIA and sit around to watch the play)

PLAYER: I am about to do a tragedy. *(acting as two players; first the king)* I am the king! *(now as brother)* And I am your brother. *(back as king)* I am tired, I think I will take a nap. *(back as brother)* I will kill him by pouring poison in his ear! Muahahaha!!! *(king dies melodramatically; back as the brother, triumphantly)* I am the new king!

CLAUDIUS: *(gets up very angrily)* STOP! Give me some light, away! Everyone, go home!

(ALL exit but HAMLET and HORATIO)

HAMLET: I was right! *(does a happy dance)*

HORATIO: Looks like it.

HAMLET: I need to see my mother! I will speak daggers to her but use none. I am MAD! MAD, I tell you!!!!

(ALL exit, HAMLET exits screaming about being mad!)

(enter CLAUDIUS)

CLAUDIUS: *(to audience)* I feel reallllllllly bad about killing my brother, King Hamlet. I think I will pray about it. Yeah, that will make me feel better! *(he kneels and starts praying; enter HAMLET)*

HAMLET: *(seeing CLAUDIUS and addressing audience)* What's this?! *(starts pulling out his sword)* And now I'll do it! And so I am revenged! But he can't fight back, so it's not fair. Oh, darn it! I hate having a conscience, it's so inconvenient! I am so confused!

(HAMLET exits)

CLAUDIUS: *(to audience)* Well, I don't know about you, but, I feel refreshed!

(CLAUDIUS exits)

(enter GERTRUDE and POLONIUS)

GERTRUDE: What's up Polonius?

POLONIUS: I am going to hide and spy on your conversation with Hamlet!

GERTRUDE: Oh, okay.

(POLONIUS hides somewhere, enter HAMLET very mad, swinging his sword around)

HAMLET: MOM!!! I AM VERY MAD!

GERTRUDE: Ahhh! You scared me!

(POLONIUS sneezes from hiding spot)

HAMLET: *(not seeing POLONIUS)* How now, a rat? Who's hiding? *(stabs POLONIUS)*

POLONIUS: O, I am slain! Ohhhh, the pain! *(dies on stage)*

GERTRUDE: Oh me, what has thou done?

HAMLET: Oops, I thought that was Claudius. Hmph, oh well... as I was saying, I AM MAD you married uncle Claudius!

GERTRUDE: Oh that, yeah, sorry. *(in a motherly voice)* Now, you just killed Polonius, clean up this mess and go to your room!

HAMLET: Okay Mom. *(mimicking his mom in her voice)* Clean up this mess and go to your room.

(ALL exit, HAMLET drags POLONIUS' body offstage)

(enter GERTRUDE and CLAUDIUS)

GERTRUDE: Ahhh, Dear?

CLAUDIUS: Yeah?

GERTRUDE: Ummmm, you would not believe what I have seen tonight! Polonius is dead.

CLAUDIUS: WHAT!?

GERTRUDE: Yeah, Hamlet was acting a little crazy, Polonius sneezed or something, then Hamlet yelled, "A rat, a rat!" and then WHACK! It was over.

CLAUDIUS: *(yelling offstage)* Rosencrantz and Guildenstern!

(enter ROSENCRANTZ & GUILDENSTERN out of breath)

ROSENCRANTZ & GUILDENSTERN: Yes sir!

CLAUDIUS: *(looking worried)* Hamlet! HAMLET! He killed Polonius!

ROSENCRANTZ: Wow!

GUILDENSTERN: Are you sure, I mean, Hamlet seems nice.

CLAUDIUS: What?! Yes, I am sure! Now, I want you to bring him here. I pray you haste in this.

ROSENCRANTZ & GUILDENSTERN: *(confused)* What?

CLAUDIUS: NOW!

ROSENCRANTZ & GUILDENSTERN: *(still confused)* Okay.

(ROSENCRANTZ & GUILDENSTERN run offstage and return with HAMLET)

CLAUDIUS: *(very casual)* Hey, what's up?

HAMLET: What noise, who calls on Hamlet? What do you want?

CLAUDIUS: Now Hamlet. Where's Polonius' body?

HAMLET: I'm not telling!

CLAUDIUS: FINE!

ROSENCRANTZ: What have you done, my lord, with the dead body?

GUILDENSTERN: Will you tell us?

HAMLET: *(sarcastically)* Suuuuuurrrrrre. It's over there. *(pointing offstage)* No, over there. *(pointing in another direction)* No! Over there! *(pointing to a random place in the audience)*

(this goes on a while and ROSENCRANTZ & GUILDENSTERN are running crazily after HAMLET'S directions all over the stage and through the audience; HAMLET is laughing at them)

GUILDENSTERN: Will you STOP! I'm tired.

CLAUDIUS: Where is Polonius?

HAMLET: Oh, all right. Up the stairs and into the lobby. *(points offstage; ROSENCRANTZ & GUILDENSTERN go get POLONIUS' body and drag him on stage)*

CLAUDIUS: Ewe... he's a mess! Hamlet, I am sending you off to England. Rosencrantz and Guildenstern, take him away!

HAMLET: Fine! Farewell, dear Mother. And I'm taking this with me! *(drags POLONIUS' body offstage)*

(ALL exit but CLAUDIUS)

CLAUDIUS: *(to audience)* I have arranged his execution in England! *(laughs evilly as he exits)* Muahahaha....

(enter HAMLET addresses audience – obviously very upset)

HAMLET: I am suddenly feeling very upset! This play is lasting really long. I need to speed this revenge thing up! Don't you all agree? *(audience will quietly answer yes)*

HAMLET: *(yelling backstage)* HEY, DO YOU ALL AGREE?

(everyone answers backstage, "YES!")

(CLAUDIUS pokes his head out)

CLAUDIUS: Ahhh, excuse me, I'm not so sure I agree....

HAMLET: *(pointing sword at CLAUDIUS)* Go away!

(ALL exit)

(enter OPHELIA and GERTRUDE)

GERTRUDE: Hey Ophelia, you feeling okay?

OPHELIA: *(acting a little crazy)* I am really feeling weird right now.

(OPHELIA wandering around stage doing weird and crazy things; enter CLAUDIUS)

CLAUDIUS: *(staring at OPHELIA)* She is acting really weird. Is she okay?

GERTRUDE: Well think about it; her father just got killed by her boyfriend, whom she just broke up with, yet is still in love with. How would you feel?

CLAUDIUS: Oh, no wonder why she is kind of wacky.

(enter LAERTES very upset)

LAERTES: Where is this king? *(noticing CLAUDIUS)* WHAT HAPPENED TO MY FATHER, *(noticing OPHELIA acting crazy)* and why is my sister looking so... loony?

GERTRUDE: Well, as I was telling Claudius, she's a bit bummed that her boyfriend killed your dad.

LAERTES: Aghhhhhhh!!! I will have REVENGE!

CLAUDIUS: Laertes, my friend, look, I will help you get your revenge. I pray you go with me.

(GERTRUDE and OPHELIA exit; SAILOR brings a letter to CLAUDIUS)

SAILOR: There's a letter for you sir. It says "Hamlet is returning!" *(SAILOR shows letter that says, "Hamlet is returning!"; SAILOR exits)*

CLAUDIUS: Listen, Hamlet killed your father and wants to kill you too!

LAERTES: Ohhhh, he thinks so! I will get him!

CLAUDIUS: Let's make an evil plan!

LAERTES: Sounds great!

(CLAUDIUS and LAERTES laugh evilly together)

CLAUDIUS: How about you and Hamlet have a sword fight? And Hamlet's sword is blunt?

LAERTES: Great! And I will put poison on my tip to make sure he dies!

CLAUDIUS: Great! And I will put poison in his drink if none of that works!

LAERTES & CLAUDIUS: GREAT!

(they high five; enter GERTRUDE)

GERTRUDE: What are you two up to?

LAERTES & CLAUDIUS: Nothing. *(laughing to each other)*

GERTRUDE: Well then, ahhh, Laertes? I have some bad news.

LAERTES: Really? I have had enough of that, can I have some good news?

GERTRUDE: Nope, Ophelia just drowned. *(GERTRUDE drags OPHELIA'S body on stage – head soaking wet if possible!)*

LAERTES: WHAT!? Drown'd! O, where?

GERTRUDE: Yeah, outside...in water...sorry.

LAERTES: Alas, then, she is drown'd?

OPHELIA: *(looks up at audience)* Drowned!

GERTRUDE: Drown'd, drown'd.

LAERTES: I am sooooo going to get Hamlet!!!!

(LAERTES runs offstage waving his sword; ALL exit GERTRUDE drags OPHELIA offstage)

(HAMLET and HORATIO enter, HAMLET finds a skull on stage)

HAMLET: Oh look, a skull.

HORATIO: Yeah, it's from this grave marked Yorick.

HAMLET: Alas, poor Yorick! I knew him, Horatio.

HORATIO: Really? Well, I think he's dead now.

HAMLET: When I was a kid, he was the jester, the funniest guy I knew.

HORATIO: Yeah? Well, he's still dead.

HAMLET: So full of life and now he's.....

HORATIO: Dead.

HAMLET: Bummer.

(enter LAERTES, GERTRUDE, and CLAUDIUS)

HORATIO: Oh look! Hide! *(HAMLET and HORATIO go off to side of stage)*

GERTRUDE: We must bury Ophelia.

LAERTES: *(starts weeping and crying extremely loud)* I AM SOOOOO MAD AT HAMLET!!! It's his fault my sister and father are dead!

(HAMLET jumps up to confront LAERTES)

HAMLET: Laertes, I loved Ophelia, how dare you say I killed her!

LAERTES: Aghhhhhh! *(charges at HAMLET and they start to fight)*

HORATIO: Hamlet, we must leave.

(HORATIO pulls back HAMLET and exits with him as HAMLET is still yelling at LAERTES; CLAUDIUS pulls back LAERTES)

(ALL exit)

(enter HAMLET and HORATIO)

HAMLET: Horatio, did you know that Rosencrantz and Guildenstern were taking me to England to have me killed!

HORATIO: Really?

HAMLET: Yeah, but I got them!

HORATIO: What did you do?

HAMLET: I tricked England into thinking that Rosencrantz and Guildenstern were to be killed.

(enter OSRIC)

HAMLET: Osric! What brings you here?

OSRIC: The king has placed a wager that you can not beat Laertes in a swordfight!

HAMLET: What!?! Bring it on!

HORATIO: I don't know man, this doesn't seem right. I will tell him you are not fit.

HAMLET: *(to OSRIC)* Tell him I will fight!

(exit OSRIC)

HORATIO: Dude, I'm telling you. This is a TRAGEDY, remember? You shouldn't fight! You will lose, my lord.

HAMLET: I don't think so. The time is NOW!

(enter LAERTES, GERTRUDE, OSRIC, CLAUDIUS, and other on-lookers)

HAMLET: So, I hear you want to fight?

LAERTES: Yeah, you killed my father... and sister, prepare to die!

HAMLET: Look, I really didn't mean to kill your father. He sneezed and freaked me out.

LAERTES: *(handing sword to HAMLET)* Just take your sword and let's go.

(CLAUDIUS and LAERTES to the side)

CLAUDIUS: Is your sword poisoned?

LAERTES: Yep. Is your wine poisoned?

CLAUDIUS: You betcha!

HORATIO: *(to HAMLET)* Listen, this doesn't seem right....

CLAUDIUS: *(to audience, while ALL watch him)* If Hamlet wins, we will all drink wine! *(winks at audience while holding up poisoned wine cup)*

(LAERTES and HAMLET start to fight, HAMLET strikes first)

LAERTES: Ouch! That hurt!

HAMLET: How about this! *(strikes him again)*

LAERTES: Hey! *(strikes back and hits HAMLET)*

HAMLET: Ouch!

GERTRUDE: All this fighting is making me thirsty! *(drinks poisoned wine)*

CLAUDIUS: GERTRUDE, do not drink! *(to audience)* It is the poisoned cup. It is too late. Oh well.

(during fight, HAMLET and LAERTES manage to drop and switch swords – this must be obvious to the audience)

LAERTES: *(to CLAUDIUS)* He has MY SWORD!

CLAUDIUS: Well, don't get hit!

(HAMLET strikes LAERTES again)

LAERTES: Noooooooooo!!!!!!!

(GERTRUDE suddenly gets up and starts to die)

HAMLET: MOMMY!!!! Aghhhhhhh!!!!

GERTRUDE: O my dear Hamlet. The drink, the drink, I am poison'd *(dies in melodramatic fashion, ALL watch)*

HAMLET: *(very mad)* Oh villainy! Ho, let the door be lock'd! Treachery! Seek it out!

(LAERTES starts dying)

LAERTES: Hamlet. Listen, Claudius poisoned the wine cup and your mom drank it. He also poisoned my sword.

HAMLET: Oh, that's not good.

HORATIO: I told you so!

LAERTES: Nope, we're both going to die. The king, the king's to blame. I am justly killed with my own treachery!

(LAERTES falls over dead)

CLAUDIUS: *(to audience)* Don't you just hate tattletales!

HAMLET: CLAUDIUS!!!! *(HAMLET chases CLAUDIUS around stage and finally kills him)*

HAMLET: *(enter FORTINBRAS and some of his men; HAMLET starting to die)* Well this did not turn out as I expected! I guess this was a tragedy after all! Fortinbras, you are now the king. O, I die. The rest is silence.

(HAMLET dies melodramatically)

FORTINBRAS: Sweet, I get to be king! *(does a happy dance, then speaks to the audience)* I like tragedies! What a mess! *(stepping over bodies)* Let's clean this up!

(ALL exit)

THE END

The 25-Minute or so Hamlet
By William Shakespeare
Creatively modified by Brendan P. Kelso
11-20+ Actors

CAST OF CHARACTERS:

HAMLET: son to the dead King Hamlet, nephew to Claudius, the thinker, or "over" thinker (he's complicated)

CLAUDIUS: the big, bad new King of Denmark

GERTRUDE: Queen, Hamlet's mom, married to his dad & then to his uncle (it's complicated)

[2]**POLONIUS:** a lord (bad guy too!)

OPHELIA: Polonius' daughter, thinks Hamlet is cute!

LAERTES: Polonius' son and sword-fighter, thinks Hamlet is rotten!

[3]**ROSENCRANTZ:** crazy guy #1

[3]**GUILDENSTERN:** crazy guy #2

HORATIO: Hamlet's closest friend

[3]**MARCELLUS:** Hamlet's friend

[3]**BARNARDO:** Hamlet's friend

[4]**GHOST:** a ghost, duh

[4]**OSRIC:** a young dude

[1]**PLAYER 1:** an actor

[1]**PLAYER 2:** another actor

[1]**GRAVEDIGGER 1:** a person who digs graves

[1]**GRAVEDIGGER 2:** see above

[2]**FORTINBRAS:** Prince of Norway

[2]**SAILOR:** a sailor

ON-LOOKERS: (extras, as many as needed)

The same actors can play the following parts:

[1]PLAYERS and GRAVEDIGGERS

[2]POLONIUS, SAILOR, and FORTINBRAS

[3]MARCELLUS & BARNARDO can play ROSENCRANTZ & GUILDENSTERN

[4]GHOST and OSRIC

(enter BARNARDO, HORATIO, and MARCELLUS)

MARCELLUS: Guys! Guess what? I have seen a ghost twice before!

HORATIO: No you haven't, have you?

BARNARDO: Yep! It's true. I have seen him too!

HORATIO: You guys are just pulling my leg!

(enter GHOST from behind HORATIO)

GHOST: *(sneaking up behind HORATIO)* Boo!

(HORATIO screaming frantically, meanwhile, MARCELLUS and BARNADO are laughing hysterically)

MARCELLUS: Is it not like the King?

BARNARDO: Yes, it looks like Hamlet's dad, just a touch more... oh, I don't know.... pale?

HORATIO: Ohhhh, that ghost is NOT a good thing. It's scary! Smells bad too. Bad things will happen! I mean, listen to his voice, it's creepy. *(GHOST makes creepy noises)*

BARNARDO: So what should we do?

HORATIO: We must tell Hamlet! He'll know what to do!

MARCELLUS and BARNARDO: Good idea!

(ALL exit)

(enter CLAUDIUS and GERTRUDE)

CLAUDIUS: *(to the audience)* I love being the ruler! *(HAMLET enters)* Hey Hamlet, my new son, why are you looking so down in the dumps?

HAMLET: *(to audience while pointing at Claudius)* A little more than kin, and less than kind. *(to Claudius)* Oh, I'm just bummed that my dad died and my mom married my uncle the very next day...ohh, excuse me...I mean YOU!

GERTRUDE: Dear, stop being such a drag. All that lives must die. You know... the circle of life, or haven't you heard?

HAMLET: Whatever Mom. That it should come to this! He is my father's brother, but no more like my father than I to Hercules! I'm going to see my friends.

(GERTRUDE, CLAUDIUS exit; HORATIO, MARCELLUS, and BARNARDO enter)

HORATIO: Hamlet, I saw your dad last night as a ghost!

HAMLET: No way!

BARNARDO and MARCELLUS: Way!

HAMLET: I thought I saw him in a dream the other night, in my mind's eye. I'll stop by tonight and check it out!

(ALL exit)

ACT 1 SCENE 3

(LAERTES, OPHELIA, and POLONIUS enter)

LAERTES: Ophelia, sis, please stop hanging out with Hamlet. That prince is a bit crazy.

OPHELIA: But I love him!

LAERTES: Whoa, remember, this is a tragedy, not a fairy tale. Most people die in tragedies, especially people who love the main character.

POLONIUS: Laertes, aren't you supposed to be going back to France?

LAERTES: Oh yeah, see ya, Dad! *(LAERTES exits)*

POLONIUS: *(to LAERTES as he leaves)* Hey! Neither a borrower nor a lender be!

LAERTES: What?

POLONIUS: Just giving you some advice about money!

LAERTES: *(a bit confused)* Oh. Okay. Later!

POLONIUS: *(to OPHELIA)* Your brother is right, Hamlet is crazy.

OPHELIA: But, I so totally like him!

POLONIUS: I forbid you to see him!

OPHELIA: I shall obey, Dad. I mean, I so totally DON'T like him anymore.

POLONIUS: Good! *(POLONIUS exits)*

OPHELIA: *(to audience)* I'm a teenager, like I'm going to listen to my dad!

(OPHELIA exits)

ACT 1 SCENES 4 & 5

(HAMLET, HORATIO, and MARCELLUS enter)

MARCELLUS: *(to the audience)* Something is rotten in the state of Denmark.

HAMLET: Okay, I'm here. Now, where is this ghost of my dad you have been talking about?

(HORATIO and MARCELLUS are looking around; GHOST enters)

HORATIO and MARCELLUS: There he is!

HAMLET: Where?

(GHOST sneaks up behind HAMLET)

GHOST: Boo!

HAMLET: Aghhhhh!

GHOST: Hah! Scared ya!

HAMLET: Who are you?

GHOST: *(in a ghostly voice)* I am your father's spirit.

HAMLET: Oh. ....What!?

GHOST: Your father, you know the ex-King! I want you to know that the serpent that did sting thy father's life now wears his crown.

HAMLET: What?

GHOST: I was the King until your Uncle Claudius poisoned me by pouring icky stuff in my ear! Murder most foul!

HAMLET: Uncle Claudius killed you?

GHOST: Yeah, then he married my wife, YOUR MOM, and then became King!

HAMLET: WHAT! Ohhh, that makes me soooo mad!

GHOST: Yeah? Well, how do you think I feel? Dead and all.... O horrible, O horrible, most horrible.

HAMLET: Yeah, guess that stinks too. So what do you want me to do?

GHOST: Avenge me! You MUST kill Claudius!

HAMLET: Whoa! Kill Claudius? Well.....ahhh....not really sure I like that, I mean, it's just not right, killing someone. What if you don't really exist?

GHOST: Did you not hear me? He killed me, married your mom, and is now the new King. Doesn't that make you a bit angry?

HAMLET: *(getting riled up)* Yeah.

GHOST: I am your father, don't you want to avenge my death!

HAMLET: *(getting more riled up)* YEAH!

GHOST: Then get going!

HAMLET: I WILL AVENGE YOU FATHER!

GHOST: Oh, and Hamlet?

HAMLET: YEAH?

GHOST: Boo! *(HAMLET jumps up scared)*

HAMLET: Quit doing that!

GHOST: Sorry son, it's one of the perks of the job. My hour is almost come, now get going! *(now in a ghostly voice)* AVENGE ME!

(GHOST exits)

HAMLET: *(to exiting ghost)* Rest, Rest, perturbed spirit!

(ALL exit)

ACT 2 SCENE 1

(enter OPHELIA and POLONIUS)

OPHELIA: Dad, Hamlet is looking a bit weird lately. I mean, his clothes are ragged and he is talking to himself...not quite as cute as he once was, but I still like him!

POLONIUS: I told you to stay away from him!

OPHELIA: I did!

POLONIUS: Hamlet is probably crazy without your love! That hath made him mad. *(to audience)* I will tell Claudius the king!

(ALL exit)

(enter CLAUDIUS, ROSENCRANTZ, GUILDENSTERN, and GERTRUDE)

CLAUDIUS: Rosencrantz and Guildenstern?

ROSENCRANTZ & GUILDENSTERN: Yes sir!

CLAUDIUS: I need you to take on a very, very, very, very, very, very secret mission!

ROSENCRANTZ: Secret mission? Yes sir!

GUILDENSTERN: We get to be spies?

ROSENCRANTZ: I want to be the spy!

GUILDENSTERN: *(starting an argument with ROSENCRANTZ)* No, I'm the spy!

ROSENCRANTZ: NO, I'm the spy!

GUILDENSTERN: NO! I'M THE SPY!

CLAUDIUS: Stop!

ROSENCRANTZ & GUILDENSTERN: Sorry sir.

GUILDENSTERN: *(whispering to ROSENCRANTZ)* I'm still the spy!

GERTRUDE: We need you to find out why Hamlet is acting so strange lately. I beseech you instantly to visit my too much changed son, Hamlet.

GUILDENSTERN: We will do whatever it takes.

ROSENCRANTZ: Hey, that's my line.

GUILDENSTERN: No, it's my line.

ROSENCRANTZ: No, It's MY line!

GUILDENSTERN: NO, IT'S MY LINE!!!

CLAUDIUS: Stop!

ROSENCRANTZ & GUILDENSTERN: Sorry, sir.

ROSENCRANTZ: By the way, is there any money in it for us?

CLAUDIUS: Sure, here's a dollar.

ROSENCRANTZ: *(takes dollar)* It's mine!

GUILDENSTERN: *(starting an argument with ROSENCRANTZ)* No, it's mine!

ROSENCRANTZ: No, mine!

GUILDENSTERN: NO! MINE!

CLAUDIUS: *(annoyed by them)* Here's another dollar, just go!

(ROSENCRANTZ & GUILDENSTERN exit still arguing; enter POLONIUS)

POLONIUS: *(to CLAUDIUS)* Sir, I have found the very cause of Hamlet's lunacy. I know why he has been acting so crazy!

GERTRUDE: Why!?

POLONIUS: I will be brief. Your noble son is mad. He is in love with Ophelia and I have told her to reject him! Claudius, why don't we spy on him?

CLAUDIUS: Sounds like fun! But what if he is faking being crazy?

POLONIUS: Hmmm. Though this be madness, yet there is method in't.

CLAUDIUS: Right?

(exit CLAUDIUS, POLONIUS, and GERTRUDE; enter HAMLET, ROSENCRANTZ & GUILDENSTERN)

ROSENCRANTZ: What's up Ham?

GUILDENSTERN: How have you been buddy?

HAMLET: Oh, just thinking.

ROSENCRANTZ: 'Bout what?

HAMLET: Well, since you asked. Did you know there is nothing either good or bad, but thinking makes it so?

GUILDENSTERN: *(ROSENCRANTZ & GUILDENSTERN looking at each other with a puzzled look on their faces)* Man, you are a weird dude.

HAMLET: Whatever. What brings you around here?

ROSENCRANTZ: My lord, we were sent for, by the king. Oh look, here come some players.

PLAYER 1: Hello. We are the players.

PLAYER 2: Here to do a play!

HAMLET: *(to audience)* Ah haa! I have an idea! The plays the thing. Wherein I'll catch the conscience of the king. I will have the players act out how my father was killed! Then Claudius will feel guilty and admit his crime! Oh, vengeance! Claudius is a bloody, bawdy villain! Remorseless, treacherous, lecherous, kindless villain! *(to PLAYERS)* Soooo, what if I said I could get you in front of the king?

PLAYER 1: Sounds great!

HAMLET: OK, but you have to do a special play that I write, you good with that?

PLAYER 2: Great! Let's go!

(ALL exit but HAMLET, who addresses audience)

HAMLET: What luck to find these actors! It will be great to see Claudius show his guilt! What a piece of work is a man! *(HAMLET exits)*

(enter HAMLET)

HAMLET: To be, or not to be, that is the question *(to audience)* Really...that *is* the question, and if any of you have the answer, I would really appreciate a little help here.

(enter OPHELIA)

OPHELIA: Hello Ham.

HAMLET: Hello O.

OPHELIA: So, whatcha been up to?

HAMLET: Just contemplating life and talking to myself again. Hey, you know I like you?

OPHELIA: Really?

HAMLET: Ahhhh, no.

OPHELIA: You are sooooo mean!

HAMLET: I don't like you at all! Get thee to a nunnery!

OPHELIA: O, woe is me! *(OPHELIA exits as she is crying with a really bad fake cry)*

HAMLET: Whatever. Now let me think of another great speech, oh yeah, *(as HAMLET exits)* What dreams may come, when we blah, blah, blah.....

(HAMLET exits)

ACT 3 SCENE 2

(enter HAMLET, PLAYERS, and HORATIO)

PLAYER 2: *(to Hamlet)* We will do the play just as you wrote it!

PLAYER 1: Do I really have to die?

PLAYER 2: Yes!

PLAYER 1: Do I get to do a great swordfight and die like a brave knight?

PLAYER 2: Ahhhh, no. You die in your sleep.

PLAYER 1: What!?!? Come on man that stinks!

PLAYER 2: Just do it. That's what the script says.

PLAYER 1: Fine, but just be warned, this may be the BEST sleep death you have EVER seen!

PLAYER 2: Fine. Let's go.

(PLAYERS off to side practicing their acting)

HAMLET: Horatio, now watch Claudius closely during the play, he will show his guilt and that will prove he killed my father! Hey guys. *(to the PLAYERS)* Suit the action to the word, the word to the action.

PLAYERS 1&2: Right!

HORATIO: Ahh, you do realize this is a tragedy, right?

HAMLET: Yeah, why?

HORATIO: Well, I just want you to know, that usually, in a tragedy, the main character gets killed in the end.

HAMLET: So what's your point?

HORATIO: YOU are the main character, they even named the play after you "HAMLET", so BE CAREFUL!

HAMLET: *(getting a little crazy)* Yeah, well, I MUST PROVE HE KILLED MY FATHER!

HORATIO: Okey-dokey. Don't say I didn't warn ya. Here they come!

(enter CLAUDIUS, GERTRUDE, OPHELIA, ROSENCRANTZ & GUILDENSTERN and sit around to watch the play)

PLAYER 2: We are about to do a tragedy.

(ROSENCRANTZ & GUILDENSTERN cheer; everyone gives them a mean look)

ROSENCRANTZ & GUILDENSTERN: Sorry.

PLAYER 1: I am the king!

PLAYER 2: I am your brother.

PLAYER 1: I am tired, I think I will take a nap. *(starts snoring very loudly)*

PLAYER 2: I will kill him by pouring poison in his ear! Muahahaha!!!

(PLAYER 1 dies melodramatically)

PLAYER 2: *(triumphantly)* I am now the king!

CLAUDIUS: *(gets up very angrily)* STOP! Give me some light, away! Everyone, go home!

(ALL exit but HAMLET and HORATIO)

HAMLET: I was right! *(does a happy dance)*

HORATIO: Looks like it.

(HAMLET off to the side to the audience)

HAMLET: I need to see my mother! I will speak daggers to her but use none. I am MAD! MAD I tell you!!!!

(ALL exit, HAMLET exits screaming about being mad!)

(enter CLAUDIUS)

CLAUDIUS: *(to audience)* I feel realllllllly bad about killing my brother, King Hamlet. I think I will pray about it. Yeah, that will make me feel better! *(he kneels and starts praying; enter HAMLET)*

HAMLET: *(seeing CLAUDIUS and addressing audience)* What's this! *(starts pulling out his sword)* And now I'll do it! And so I am revenged! But he can't fight back, so it's not fair. Oh, darn it! I hate having a conscience, it's so inconvenient! I am so confused!

(HAMLET exits)

CLAUDIUS: *(to audience)* Well, I don't know about you, but, I feel refreshed!

(CLAUDIUS exits)

(enter GERTRUDE and POLONIUS)

GERTRUDE: What's up Polonius?

POLONIUS: I am going to hide and spy on your conversation with Hamlet!

GERTRUDE: Oh, okay.

(POLONIUS hides somewhere, enter HAMLET very mad, swinging his sword around)

HAMLET: MOM!!! I AM VERY MAD!

GERTRUDE: Ahhh! You scared me!

(POLONIUS sneezes from hiding spot)

HAMLET: *(not seeing POLONIUS)* How now, a rat? Who's hiding? *(stabs POLONIUS)*

POLONIUS: O, I am slain! Ohhhh, the pain! *(dies on stage)*

GERTRUDE: Oh me, what has thou done?

HAMLET: Oops, I thought that was Claudius. Hmph, oh well... as I was saying, I AM MAD you married uncle Claudius!

GERTRUDE: Oh that, yeah, sorry. *(in a motherly voice)* Now, you just killed Polonius, clean up this mess and go to your room!

HAMLET: Okay Mom. *(mimicking his mom in her voice)* Clean up this mess and go to your room.

(ALL exit, HAMLET drags POLONIUS' body offstage)

(enter GERTRUDE and CLAUDIUS)

GERTRUDE: Ahhh, Dear?

CLAUDIUS: Yeah?

GERTRUDE: Ummmm, you would not believe what I have seen tonight! Polonius is dead.

CLAUDIUS: WHAT!?

GERTRUDE: Yeah, Hamlet was acting a little crazy, Polonius sneezed or something, then Hamlet yelled, "A rat, a rat!" and then WHACK! It was over.

CLAUDIUS: *(yelling offstage)* Rosencrantz and Guildenstern!

(enter ROSENCRANTZ & GUILDENSTERN out of breath)

ROSENCRANTZ & GUILDENSTERN: Yes sir!

CLAUDIUS: *(looking worried)* Hamlet! HAMLET! He killed Polonius!

ROSENCRANTZ: Wow!

GUILDENSTERN: Are you sure, I mean, Hamlet seems nice.

CLAUDIUS: What?! Yes, I am sure! Now, I want you to bring him here. I pray you haste in this.

ROSENCRANTZ & GUILDENSTERN: *(confused)* What?

CLAUDIUS: NOW!

ROSENCRANTZ & GUILDENSTERN: *(still confused)* Okay.

(ROSENCRANTZ & GUILDENSTERN run offstage and return with HAMLET)

CLAUDIUS: *(very casual)* Hey, what's up?

HAMLET: What noise, who calls on Hamlet? What do you want?

CLAUDIUS: Now Hamlet. Where's Polonius' body?

HAMLET: I'm not telling!

CLAUDIUS: FINE!

ROSENCRANTZ: What have you done, my lord, with the dead body?

GUILDENSTERN: Will you tell us?

HAMLET: *(sarcastically)* Suuuuuurrrrrre. It's over there. *(pointing offstage)* No, over there. *(pointing in another direction)* No! Over there! *(pointing to a random place in the audience)*

(this goes on a while and ROSENCRANTZ & GUILDENSTERN are running crazily after HAMLET'S directions all over the stage and through the audience; HAMLET is laughing at them)

GUILDENSTERN: Will you STOP! I'm tired.

CLAUDIUS: Where is Polonius?

HAMLET: Oh, all right. Up the stairs and into the lobby. *(points offstage; ROSENCRANTZ & GUILDENSTERN go get POLONIUS' body and drag him on stage)*

CLAUDIUS: Ewe... he's a mess! Hamlet, I am sending you off to England. Rosencrantz and Guildenstern, take him away!

HAMLET: Fine! Farewell, dear Mother. And I'm taking this with me! *(drags POLONIUS' body offstage)*

(ALL exit but CLAUDIUS)

CLAUDIUS: *(to audience)* I have arranged his execution in England! *(laughs evilly as he exits)* Muahahaha....

(enter HAMLET addresses audience – obviously very upset)

HAMLET: I am suddenly feeling very upset! This play is lasting really long. I need to speed this revenge thing up! Don't you all agree? *(audience will quietly answer yes)*

HAMLET: *(yelling backstage)* HEY, DO YOU ALL AGREE?

(everyone answers backstage, "YES!")

(CLAUDIUS pokes his head out)

CLAUDIUS: Ahhh, excuse me, I'm not so sure I agree....

HAMLET: *(pointing sword at CLAUDIUS)* Go away!

(ALL exit)

(enter OPHELIA and GERTRUDE)

GERTRUDE: Hey Ophelia, you feeling okay?

OPHELIA: *(acting a little crazy)* I am really feeling weird right now.

(OPHELIA wandering around stage doing weird and crazy things; enter CLAUDIUS)

CLAUDIUS: *(staring at OPHELIA)* She is acting really weird. Is she okay?

GERTRUDE: Well think about it; her father just got killed by her boyfriend, whom she just broke up with, yet is still in love with. How would you feel?

CLAUDIUS: Oh, no wonder why she is kind of wacky.

(enter LAERTES very upset)

LAERTES: Where is this king? *(noticing CLAUDIUS)* WHAT HAPPENED TO MY FATHER, *(noticing OPHELIA acting crazy)* and why is my sister looking so... loony?

GERTRUDE: Well, as I was telling Claudius, she's a bit bummed that her boyfriend killed your dad.

LAERTES: Aghhhhhhh!!! I will have REVENGE!

CLAUDIUS: Laertes, my friend, look, I will help you get your revenge. I pray you go with me.

(GERTRUDE and OPHELIA exit; SAILOR brings a letter to CLAUDIUS)

SAILOR: There's a letter for you sir. It says "Hamlet is returning!" *(SAILOR shows letter that says, "Hamlet is returning!"; SAILOR exits)*

CLAUDIUS: Listen, Hamlet killed your father and wants to kill you too!

LAERTES: Ohhhh, he thinks so! I will get him!

CLAUDIUS: Let's make an evil plan!

LAERTES: Sounds great!

(CLAUDIUS and LAERTES laugh evilly together)

CLAUDIUS: How about you and Hamlet have a sword fight? And Hamlet's sword is blunt?

LAERTES: Great! And I will put poison on my tip to make sure he dies!

CLAUDIUS: Great! And I will put poison in his drink if none of that works!

LAERTES & CLAUDIUS: GREAT!

(they high five; enter GERTRUDE)

GERTRUDE: What are you two up to?

LAERTES & CLAUDIUS: Nothing. *(laughing to each other)*

GERTRUDE: Well then, ahhh, Laertes? I have some bad news.

LAERTES: Really? I have had enough of that, can I have some good news?

GERTRUDE: Nope, Ophelia just drowned. *(GERTRUDE drags OPHELIA'S body on stage – head soaking wet if possible!)*

LAERTES: WHAT!? Drown'd! O, where?

GERTRUDE: Yeah, outside...in water...sorry.

LAERTES: Alas, then, she is drown'd?

OPHELIA: *(looks up at audience)* Drowned!

GERTRUDE: Drown'd, drown'd.

LAERTES: I am sooooo going to get Hamlet!!!!

(LAERTES runs offstage waving his sword; ALL exit GERTRUDE drags OPHELIA offstage)

ACT 5 SCENE 1

(enter GRAVEDIGGERS; HAMLET and HORATIO are off to the side watching gravediggers)

GRAVEDIGGER 1: You know, I really have to get a better job! Digging graves is no way to make a living! Get it? Graves – living? *(starts laughing to himself)*

GRAVEDIGGER 2: Yeah. I get that your jokes are really bad. Oh, look what I found, a skull from this grave called Yorick.

(HAMLET jumps up and grabs skull; GRAVEDIGGERS exit)

HAMLET: Alas, poor Yorick! I knew him, Horatio.

HORATIO: Really? Well, I think he's dead now.

HAMLET: When I was a kid, he was the jester, the funniest guy I knew.

HORATIO: Yeah? Well, he's still dead.

HAMLET: So full of life and now he's.....

HORATIO: Dead.

HAMLET: Bummer.

(enter LAERTES, GERTRUDE, and CLAUDIUS)

HORATIO: Oh look! Hide! *(HAMLET and HORATIO go off to side of stage)*

GERTRUDE: We must bury Ophelia.

LAERTES: *(starts weeping and crying extremely loud)* I AM SOOOOO MAD AT HAMLET!!! It's his fault my sister and father are dead!

(HAMLET jumps up to confront LAERTES)

HAMLET: Laertes, I loved Ophelia, how dare you say I killed her!

LAERTES: Aghhhhhh! *(charges at HAMLET and they start to fight)*

HORATIO: Hamlet, we must leave.

(HORATIO pulls back HAMLET and exits with him as HAMLET is still yelling at LAERTES; CLAUDIUS pulls back LAERTES)

(ALL exit)

ACT 5 SCENE 2

(enter HAMLET and HORATIO)

HAMLET: Horatio, did you know that Rosencrantz and Guildenstern were taking me to England to have me killed!

HORATIO: Really?

HAMLET: Yeah, but I got them!

HORATIO: What did you do?

HAMLET: I tricked England into thinking that Rosencrantz and Guildenstern were to be killed.

(enter ROSENCRANTZ & GUILDENSTERN)

ROSENCRANTZ: WHAT?!

GUILDENSTERN: We're dead?

HAMLET: Yep!

ROSENCRANTZ & GUILDENSTERN: *(looking at each other)* Well that stinks. *(both suddenly die dramatically on stage)*

(enter OSRIC stepping over bodies)

HAMLET: Osric! What brings you here?

OSRIC: The king has placed a wager that you can not beat Laertes in a swordfight!

HAMLET: What!?! Bring it on!

HORATIO: I don't know man, this doesn't seem right. I will tell him you are not fit.

HAMLET: *(to OSRIC)* Tell him I will fight!

(exit OSRIC)

HORATIO: Dude, I'm telling you. This is a TRAGEDY, remember? You shouldn't fight! You will lose, my lord.

HAMLET: I don't think so. The time is NOW!

(enter LAERTES, GERTRUDE, OSRIC, CLAUDIUS, and other on-lookers)

HAMLET: So, I hear you want to fight?

LAERTES: Yeah, you killed my father... and sister, prepare to die!

HAMLET: Look, I really didn't mean to kill your father. He sneezed and freaked me out.

LAERTES: *(handing sword to HAMLET)* Just take your sword and let's go.

(CLAUDIUS and LAERTES to the side)

CLAUDIUS: Is your sword poisoned?

LAERTES: Yep. Is your wine poisoned?

CLAUDIUS: You betcha!

HORATIO: *(to HAMLET)* Listen, this doesn't seem right....

CLAUDIUS: *(to audience, while ALL watch him)* If Hamlet wins, we will all drink wine! *(winks at audience while holding up poisoned wine cup)*

(LAERTES and HAMLET start to fight, HAMLET strikes first)

LAERTES: Ouch! That hurt!

HAMLET: How about this! *(strikes him again)*

LAERTES: Hey! *(strikes back and hits HAMLET)*

HAMLET: Ouch!

GERTRUDE: All this fighting is making me thirsty! *(drinks poisoned wine)*

CLAUDIUS: GERTRUDE, do not drink! *(to audience)* It is the poisoned cup. It is too late. Oh well.

(during fight, HAMLET and LAERTES manage to drop and switch swords – this must be obvious to the audience)

LAERTES: *(to CLAUDIUS)* He has MY SWORD!

CLAUDIUS: Well, don't get hit!

(HAMLET strikes LAERTES again)

LAERTES: Noooooooooo!!!!!!!

(GERTRUDE suddenly gets up and starts to die)

HAMLET: MOMMY!!!! Aghhhhhhh!!!!

GERTRUDE: O my dear Hamlet. The drink, the drink, I am poison'd *(dies in melodramatic fashion, ALL watch)*

HAMLET: *(very mad)* Oh villainy! Ho, let the door be lock'd! Treachery! Seek it out!

(LAERTES starts dying)

LAERTES: Hamlet. Listen, Claudius poisoned the wine cup and your mom drank it. He also poisoned my sword.

HAMLET: Oh, that's not good.

HORATIO: I told you so!

LAERTES: Nope, we're both going to die. The king, the king's to blame. I am justly killed with my own treachery!

(LAERTES falls over dead)

CLAUDIUS: *(to audience)* Don't you just hate tattletales!

HAMLET: CLAUDIUS!!!! *(HAMLET chases CLAUDIUS around stage and finally kills him)*

HAMLET: *(enter FORTINBRAS and some of his men; HAMLET starting to die)* Well this did not turn out as I expected! I guess this was a tragedy after all! Fortinbras, you are now the king. O, I die. The rest is silence.

(HAMLET dies melodramatically)

FORTINBRAS: Sweet, I get to be king! *(does a happy dance)* I like tragedies! What a mess! *(stepping over bodies)* Oh look, Rosencrantz and Guildenstern are dead too. Let's clean this up!

(ALL exit)

THE END

Special Thanks

Special thanks to Debra Williamson, whose humorous constructive criticism is, well... greatly appreciated!

Also, I have directed this version of Hamlet to well over 20 different groups and classes, and each time some kid points out something I missed or a funnier way to say or present a line. Throughout the years, I have incorporated these modifications into this play. So, there is not one specific kid, but all the kids I have to thank for being so creative in the process! THAT'S what it's all about! THANK YOU!!!

Sneak Peeks at other Playing With Plays books:

The Three Musketeers for Kids

(ATHOS and D'ARTAGNAN enter)

ATHOS: Glad you could make it. I have engaged two of my friends as seconds.

D'ARTAGNAN: Seconds?

ATHOS: Yeah, they make sure we fight fair. Oh, here they are now!

(enter ARAMIS and PORTHOS singing, "Bad boys, bad boys, watcha gonna do...")

PORTHOS: Hey! I'm fighting him in an hour. I am going to fight... because...well... I am going to fight!

ARAMIS: And I fight him at two o'clock! Ours is a theological quarrel. *(does a thinking pose)*

D'ARTAGNAN: Yeah, yeah, yeah... I'll get to you soon!

ATHOS: We are the Three Musketeers; Athos, Porthos, and Aramis.

D'ARTAGNAN: Whatever, Ethos, Pathos, and Logos, let's just finish this! *(swords crossed and are about to fight; enter JUSSAC and cardinal's guards)*

PORTHOS: The cardinal's guards! Sheathe your swords, gentlemen.

JUSSAC: Dueling is illegal! You are under arrest!

ARAMIS: *(to ATHOS and PORTHOS)* There are five of them and we are but three.

D'ARTAGNAN: *(steps forward to join them)* It appears to me we are four! I have the spirit; my heart is that of a Musketeer.

PORTHOS: Great! I love fighting!

(Musketeers say "Fight, fight fight!...Fight, fight, fight!" as they are fighting; D'ARTAGNAN fights JUSSAC and it's the big fight; JUSSAC is wounded and exits; the 3 MUSKETEERS cheer)

ATHOS: Well done! Let's go see Treville and the king!

ARAMIS: And we don't have to kill you now!

PORTHOS: And let's get some food, too! I'm hungry!

D'ARTAGNAN: *(to audience)* This is fun!

(ALL exit)

ACT 2 SCENE 1

(enter 3 MUSKETEERS, D'ARTAGNAN, and TREVILLE)

TREVILLE: The king wants to see you, and he's not too happy you killed a few of the cardinal's guards.

(enter KING)

KING: *(yelling)* YOU GUYS HUMILIATED THE CARDINAL'S GUARDS!

ATHOS: Sire, they attacked us!

KING: Oh...Well then, bravo! I hear D'Artagnan beat the cardinal's best swordsman! Brave young man! Here's some money for you. Enjoy! *(hands money to D'ARTAGNAN)*

D'ARTAGNAN: Sweet!

(ALL exit)

PlayingWithPlays.com

Richard III for Kids
ACT 1 SCENE 4

(CLARENCE is in prison, sleeping; he wakes up from a bad dream)

CLARENCE: Terrible, horrible, no good, very bad dream! *(pauses, notices audience and addresses them)* O, I have pass'd a miserable night! I dreamt that Richard was trying to kill me! Hahahaha, Richard is SUCH a good guy, he would NEVER do a thing like that!

(enter MURDERER carrying a weapon)

MURDERER: I sounded like such a pro, no one will know it's my first day on the job! Hehehe!

CLARENCE: Hey! Who's there?

MURDERER: Um... um... *(hides his murder weapon behind his back)*

CLARENCE: Your eyes do menace me. Are you planning to murder me? 'Cause that's not a good idea. My brother Richard is a REALLY powerful guy.

MURDERER: Ha! Richard is the one who sent me here to do this! *(a pause)* Whoops...

CLARENCE: Hahaha, you foolish fellow. Richard loves me.

MURDERER: Dude, what are you not getting? He PAID me to do this!

CLARENCE: O, do not slander him, for he is kind.

(The MURDERER stabs CLARENCE; CLARENCE dies a dramatic death)

CLARENCE: Kinda ruthless... *(dies)*

MURDERER: *(Gasps)* Oh, my! He's dead! I feel bad now... I bet Clarence was a really nice guy. Ahhh, the guilt! Wow, I should have stayed in clown school.

(MURDERER exits)

ACT 2 SCENE 1

(KING EDWARD is surrounded by QUEEN ELIZABETH and BUCKINGHAM)

KING EDWARD: Well, this has been a great day at work! Everyone's agreed to get along!

(ELIZABETH and BUCKINGHAM shake hands with each other to celebrate the peace; enter RICHARD; KING EDWARD smiles happily)

KING EDWARD: If I die, I will be at peace! But I must say I'm feeling a lot healthier after all of this peace-making!

RICHARD: Hey! Looks like you're all in a good mood. That's great, 'cause you know I LOVE getting along! So what's up?

KING EDWARD: I made them like each other!

RICHARD: How lovely! I like you all now, too! Group hug? *(everyone shakes their head)* No? *(he grins sweetly)*

ELIZABETH: Wonderful! Once Clarence gets back from the Tower, everything will be perfect!

RICHARD: WHAT??? We make peace and then you insult us like this? That's no way to talk about a DEAD man!!

(EVERYONE gasps)

KING EDWARD: Is Clarence dead? I told them to cancel the execution!

RICHARD: Oh, yeah... guess that was too late! *(winks to audience)*

KING EDWARD: Nooooooo!!!! Oh my poor brother! Now I feel more sick than EVER! Oh, poor Clarence!

(All exit except RICHARD and BUCKINGHAM)

RICHARD: Well, that sure worked as planned!

BUCKINGHAM: Great job, partner!

(both exit, laughing evilly)

Treasure Island
for Kids

(enter JIM, TRELAWNEY, and DOCTOR; enter CAPTAIN SMOLLETT from the other side of the stage)

TRELAWNEY: Hello Captain. Are we all shipshape and seaworthy?

CAPTAIN: Trelawney, I don't know what you're thinking, but I don't like this cruise; and I don't like the men.

TRELAWNEY: *(very angry)* Perhaps you don't like the ship?

CAPTAIN: Nope, I said it short and sweet.

DOCTOR: What? Why?

CAPTAIN: Because I heard we are going on a treasure hunt and the coordinates of the island are: *(whispers to DOCTOR)*

DOCTOR: Wow! That's exactly right!

CAPTAIN: There's been too much blabbing already.

DOCTOR: Right! But, I doubt ANYTHING will go wrong!

CAPTAIN: Fine. Let's sail!

(ALL exit)

Act 2 Scene 3

(enter JIM, SILVER, and various other pirates)

SILVER: Ay, ay, mates. You know the song: Fifteen men on the dead man's chest.

ALL PIRATES: Yo-ho-ho and a bottle of rum!

(PIRATES slowly exit)

JIM: *(to the audience)* So, the Hispaniola had begun her voyage to the Isle of Treasure. As for Long John, well, he still is the nicest cook...

SILVER: Do you want a sandwich?

JIM: That would be great, thanks Long John! *(SILVER exits; JIM addresses audience)* As you can see, Long John is a swell guy! Until...

(JIM hides in the corner)

Act 2 Scene 4

(enter SILVER and OTHER PIRATES)

JIM: *(to audience)* I overheard Long John talking to the rest of the pirates.

SILVER: Listen here you, Scallywags! I was with Captain Flint when he hid this treasure. And those cowards have the map. Follow my directions, and no killing, yet. Clear?

DICK: Clear.

SILVER: But, when we do kill them, I claim Trelawney. And remember, dead men don't bite.

GEORGE: Ay, ay, Long John!

(ALL exit but JIM)

JIM: *(to audience)* Oh no! Long John Silver IS the one-legged man that Billy Bones warned me about! I have to tell the others!

(JIM runs offstage)

Henry V for Kids

ACT 2 SCENE 2

(enter BEDFORD and EXETER, observing CAMBRIDGE and SCROOP, who whisper among themselves)

BEDFORD: Hey Exeter, do you think it's a good idea that King Henry is letting those conspirators wander around freely?

EXETER: It's alright, Bedford. King Henry has a plan! He knows EVERYTHING they are plotting. BUT, they don't KNOW he knows. And HE knows that they don't know he knows...and...

BEDFORD: *(interrupting)* Okay, okay, I get it. Let's go sit in the audience and watch! *(they sit in the audience; enter HENRY)*

HENRY: Greetings, my good and FAITHFUL friends, Cambridge and Scroop. Perfect timing! I need your advice on something.

CAMBRIDGE: Sure thing. You know we'd do anything for you! Never was a monarch better feared and loved.

SCROOP: That's why we're going to kick some French butt!! *(SCROOP and CAMBRIDGE high-five)*

HENRY: Excellent! A man was arrested yesterday for shouting nasty things about me. But I'm sure by now he's thought better of it. I think I ought to show mercy and pardon him.

SCROOP: Nah, let him be punished.

HENRY: Ahhh, but let us yet be merciful.

CAMBRIDGE: Nah, I'm with Scroop! Off with his head!

HENRY: Is that your final answer?

CAMBRIDGE & SCROOP: YES!

HENRY: Ok, but if we don't show mercy for small offenses, how will we show mercy for big ones? I will release him. Now, take a look at THESE LETTERS.

(as CAMBRIDGE and SCROOP read the letters, their jaws drop)

HENRY: Why, how now, gentlemen? What see you in those papers that your jaws hang so low?

EXETER: *(to audience)* The letters betray their guilt!

CAMBRIDGE: I do confess my fault...

SCROOP:...and do submit me to your Highness' mercy! *(they start begging and pleading on the ground)*

HENRY: Exeter, Bedford, arrest these traitors. What did they say... Oh yeah, OFF WITH THEIR HEADS!

CAMBRIDGE: Whoa there!

SCROOP: Off with our what? What happened to the whole "mercy" thing you were just talking about!?

HENRY: Your own words talked me out of it! Take them away!

CAMBRIDGE: Well, this stinks!

(EXETER and BEDFORD arrest CAMBRIDGE and SCROOP; ALL exit, except HENRY)

HENRY: Being king is no fun sometimes. Scroop used to be one of my best friends. *(SCROOP runs on stage and dies melodramatically)* But there's no time to mope! *(CAMBRIDGE runs on stage and dies on top of SCROOP)* The signs of war advance. No king of England, if not King of France! NOW CLEAN UP THIS MESS!

(EXETER and BEDFORD run on stage and drag bodies off; exit HENRY)

King Lear for Kids

ACT 1 SCENE 1

KING LEAR's palace

(enter FOOL entertaining the audience with jokes, dancing, juggling, Hula Hooping... whatever the actor's skill may be; enter KENT)

KENT: Hey, Fool!

FOOL: What did you call me?!

KENT: I called you Fool.

FOOL: That's my name, don't wear it out! *(to audience)* Seriously, that's my name in the play!

(enter LEAR, CORNWALL, ALBANY, GONERIL, REGAN, and CORDELIA)

LEAR: The lords of France and Burgundy are outside. They both want to marry you, Cordelia.

ALL: Ooooooo!

LEAR: *(to audience)* Between you and me she IS my favorite child! *(to the girls)* Daughters, I need to talk to you about something. It's a really big deal.

GONERIL & REGAN: Did you buy us presents?

LEAR: This is even better than presents!

GONERIL & REGAN: Goody, goody!!!

CORDELIA: Father, your love is enough for me.

LEAR: Give me the map there, Kent. Girls, I'm tired. I've made a decision: Know that we - and by 'we' I mean 'me' - have divided in three our kingdom...

KENT: Whoa! Sir, dividing the kingdom may cause chaos! People could die!

FOOL: Well, this IS a tragedy...

LEAR: You worry too much, Kent. I'm giving it to my daughters so their husbands can be rich and powerful... like me!

CORNWALL & ALBANY: Sweet!

GONERIL & REGAN: Wait... what?

CORDELIA: This is olden times. That means that everything we own belongs to our husbands.

GONERIL & REGAN: Olden times stink!

CORDELIA: Truth.

LEAR: So, my daughters, tell your daddy how much you love him. Goneril, our eldest-born, speak first.

GONERIL: Sir, I love you more than words can say! More than outer space, puppies and cotton candy! I love you more than any child has ever loved a father in the history of the entire world, dearest Pops!

CORDELIA: *(to audience)* Holy moly! Surely, he won't be fooled by that. *(to self)* Love, and be silent.

LEAR: Thanks, sweetie! I'm giving you this big chunk of the kingdom here. What says our second daughter, Our dearest Regan, wife to Cornwall? Speak.

REGAN: What she said, Daddy... times a thousand!

CORDELIA: *(to audience)* What?! I love my father more than either of them. But I can't express it in words. My love's more richer than my tongue.

LEAR: Wow, Regan! You get this big hunk of the kingdom. Cordelia, what can you tell me to get this giant piece of kingdom as your own? Speak.

CORDELIA: Nothing, my lord.

LEAR: Nothing?!?

CORDELIA: Nothing.

LEAR: Come on, now. Nothing will come of nothing.

CORDELIA: I love you as a daughter loves her father.

LEAR: Try a little, harder, sweetie!

CORDELIA: Why are my sisters married if they give you all their love?

LEAR: How did you get so mean?

CORDELIA: Father, I will not insult you by telling you my love is like... as big as a whale.

LEAR: *(getting mad)* Fine. I'll split your share between your sisters.

REGAN, GONERIL, & CORNWALL: Yessss!

KENT: Whoa! Let's all just calm down a minute!

LEAR: Peace, Kent! You don't want to mess with me right now. I told you she was my favorite...

GONERIL & REGAN: What!?

LEAR: ...and she can't even tell me she loves me more than a whale? Nope. Now I'm mad.

KENT: Royal Lear, really...

LEAR: Kent, I'm pretty emotional right now! You better not try to talk me out of this...

KENT: Sir, you're acting ... insane.

BRENDAN P. KELSO, came to writing modified Shakespeare scripts when he was taking time off from work to be at home with his newly born son. "It just grew from there". Within months, he was being asked to offer classes in various locations and acting organizations along the Central Coast of California. Originally employed as an engineer, Brendan never thought about writing. However, his unique personality, humor, and love for engaging the kids with The Bard has led him to leave the engineering world and pursue writing as a new adventure in life! He has always believed, "the best way to learn is to have fun!" Brendan makes his home on the Central Coast of California and loves to spend time with his wife and son.

CAST AUTOGRAPHS